CLEO HEARN:
MR. BLACK RODEO

Elizabeth Ann Lawless

Illustrations: Hatice Bayramoglu

CLEO HEARN: MR. BLACK COWBOY

Co-Published by Wild West Diversity & Adriel Publishing

FIRST EDITION

Cover design by Hatice Bayramoglu and Elizabeth Ann Lawless

Printed in the U.S.A.

ISBN: 978-1-892324-84-9

www.WildWestDiversity.com

www.CowboysOfColorRodeo.com

This book is dedicated to
all the boys and girls
who dream of being a
professional cowboy or cowgirl.

If Cleo did it!

You can too!

DREAMING OF BEING A COWBOY

Recently a neighbor told Cleo,
"I remember when you were just a
little boy riding your stick horse up
and down the sidewalk.
And, look at you now all these years
living the life of a real professional cowboy.
I am so proud of you and
your cowboy legacy."

One day Cleo's cousin took him to the Rodeo and
he met a Black Cowboy for the
very first time.

Marvel Rodgers shook his hand and
made him feel ten feet tall.

Marvel became his hero. Cleo decided he wanted
to be a professional cowboy just like Marvel.

Cleo started dreaming of being a Professional Rodeo Cowboy like Marvel Rogers and the other Black Cowboys he met at his first all Black Rodeo in Oakmulgee, Oklahoma.

He thought it was so cool that Marvel would puff out a smoke ring every time the horses feet hit the ground.

Cleo fell in love with horses, but his family didn't have horses. He made up his mind that day to find a way to be near them.

Cleo found a ranch that was two miles from his house and he would walk there whenever he could.

There was this big beautiful tan horse and Cleo told the horse, "*We are going to be good friends one day soon.*"

The horse looked at him funny, but Cleo was determined to make his dream of riding and roping come true.

Cleo started going to the ranch after school and on weekends. He just wanted to get to know the horse.

"Who is this small cowboy and what does he want from me.
It almost seemed like he was trying to convince me to be friends.
I always liked kids so I didn't really need to be convinced."

Being around horses made Cleo so happy. After one visit, the horse finally let Cleo ride him.

Day after day Cleo and the horse would ride around the paddock and then the ranch ... getting to know each other.

"I will be a famous rodeo cowboy one day," Cleo told his friend the horse.

Riding in his first rodeo ...

Although Cleo tried bull riding and steer wrestling
when he first started rodeoing,
tie-down calf roping became his
favorite event and he vowed to be the
best calf roper he could be.

His dream was to join the Professional
Rodeo Association and win a
National Championship when he got older.

Cleo went to college on a Rodeo Scholarship but then they cancelled the College Rodeo team; he was so mad he quit school.

Since he wasn't in school, he got drafted by the Army. He called his mother and said, *"There must be some mistake."* And she said, *"Yes and you made it. I told you to stay in school."*

He doesn't know how it happened, but he got the last – but best assignment.

Cleo was chosen to be one of the first eight African American's to serve in the Presidential Honor Guard under President John F. Kennedy. Kennedy was a great guy and they became good friends.

Standing at the tomb of the unknown soldier was the most humbling and proudest moment of Cleo's service in the Army.

However, he knew he needed a degree for his future, so he left the Army when his time was up to go back to college.

HERE RESTS IN
HONORED GLORY
AN AMERICAN
SOLDIER

During his Army and college days Cleo continued to rodeo and then he graduate from Langston University in Oklahoma.

His first commercial was with Ford Tractor. They were looking for a Black Cowboy and they saw Cleo at a rodeo. *"You never know where an opportunity will lead you,"* Cleo tells people.

He joined the Ford Tractor Sales Team when they found out he had a Business Degree, so things worked out great for him.

He eventually moved to Ford Motor Company and sold trucks. But Cleo always went to a rodeo every weekend when he could.

Then he was asked to produce his first rodeo even though he wasn't a rodeo producer.

Taking a 100 Black Cowboys to Harlem, New York in 1971 was a proud moment for him and his Black Cowboy friends Bud Bramwell, Rufus Green, Sr., Myrtis Dightman and all of the guys from Texas and Oklahoma.

It was hard at first because Cleo couldn't always ride in the rodeo arena in front of the crowds because of the color of his skin.
But eventually his fast tie-down time made the rodeo producers take notice.

Tie-down calf roping gave him a lot of pleasure and he continued to practice so he would be ready for the big rodeo events.

In 1970, Cleo became the first African American to win a National Tie-Down Calf Roping Championship when he competed at The National Western in Denver, Colorado.

His boys were growing up and they had wonderful summer trips going to rodeos across the country. Cleo was glad they were getting this education of seeing new things and meeting people from all walks of life.

He was so proud that all of them wanted to be professional cowboys.

They got a lot of strange looks when they attended rodeos around the country, but eventually they gained respect because of their work ethic, athletic skills and fast tie-down times.

Cleo wanted to help his boys and younger cowboys, so the road wouldn't be as hard as it was for him.

So in 1985, when the African American Museum Dallas asked him to put on a Rodeo as a fundraiser ... he said, "Yes!"

Cleo figured this was a way to give younger cowboys an opportunity. He also wanted to share his love for the sport, tell a true inclusive history and expose the audience to the Black Western lifestyle.

Cleo continued to go to the Rodeo in Wyoming, Texas, Oklahoma, and many other places where he won lots of buckles, saddles and money.

His boys all went to college on rodeo scholarships, got good jobs and worked with him to produce Cowboys of Color Rodeos.

They created a 7-City Tour and produced rodeos in Oklahoma City, Austin, San Antonio, Dallas, Houston, Fort Worth, and Mesquite.

Then the grandchildren started riding when they came along. The family put them on horses when they were just babies and they competed in junior rodeo events into their teen and now adult lives.

Taylor competed in junior tie-down calf roping and Rachel competed in junior barrel racing. They made the family proud.

Today, Taylor pitches for the Texas Rangers and Rachel still competes in rodeos.

Now the great grandchildren are participating so they can carry on the Hearn Family Rodeo legacy.

Charles Flores Hearn practices weekly so he can compete in Saddle Bronc Riding at Fort Worth, Texas and other rodeos.

Charles is also the Director of Social Media for Cowboys of Color Rodeo and Wild West Diversity.

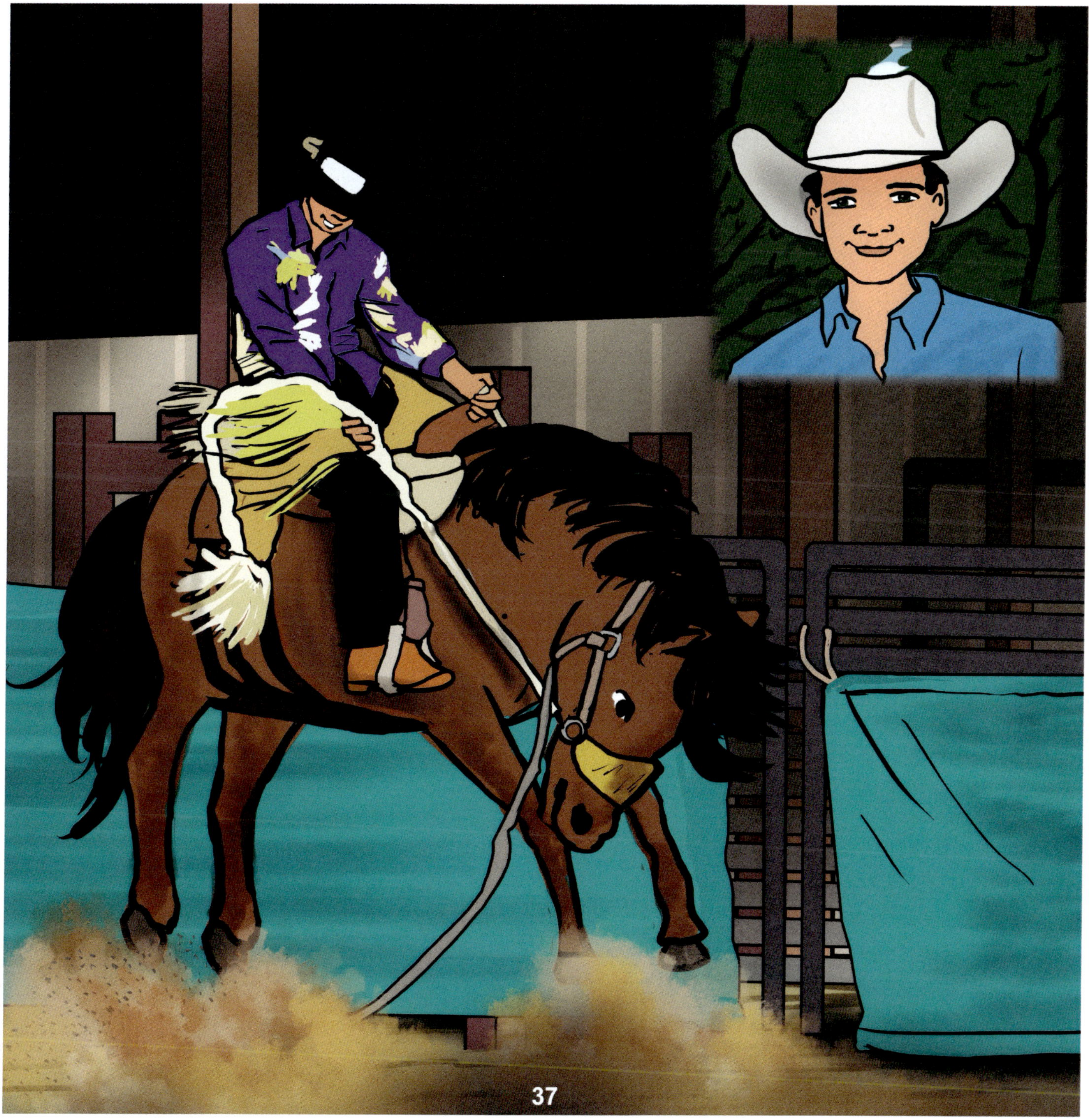

The 50 year legacy of the Hearn Family Rodeo has taught the history of minority cowboys and cowgirls while offering rodeo opportunity for the next generation.

Cleo is so happy his four sons: Harlan, Eldon, Robby and Wendell along with the grandchildren and great grandchildren are continuing their family rodeo legacy.

May it continue for another 50 years!

"To be happy in life ... all you need is something to love, something to do and something to look forward to" Cleo says.

Rodeo has been that for him and his family.

Now in his mid-80's he can say

HE LIVED HIS DREAM

OF BEING A

PROFESSIONAL RODEO COWBOY!

The author is grateful for the 30 years she has been able to work as Cleo's assistant and to help tell these wonderful stories of multicultural contributions to rodeo and the settling of the American Wild West.

For more stories visit
www.CowboysOfColorRodeo.com
or subscribe to our YouTube Channel
@WildWestDiversity

Elizabeth Ann Lawless

Creator • Entrepreneur • Author • Host

Liz is the author of fifteen books the most recent ones, *"Cleo Hearn: Mr. Black Rodeo"* and *"African American Western Legends: Yesterday."* She is the founder and host of Wild West Diversity Publishing, Livestreaming and Podcasting. For 30 years she has served as the Publicist/Historian for Cowboys of Color Rodeos, the largest multicultural rodeo in the country. Liz also speaks about *"Western Legends: Yesterday & Today"* and *"The Economic Impact of Black Cowboys: Yesterday & Today"* on livestreams, podcasts and as a speaker at libraries, PreK-12 schools, social studies conferences, colleges, and summer camp programs.

You can follow Liz at

www.Linkedin.com/in/lawlessliz

www.Facebook.com/wildwestdiversity

or join our free newsletter at

www.WildWestDiversity.com

Made in the USA
Coppell, TX
03 July 2026

83480353R00029